THE PILOT'S DAUGHTER

Books by
GARDNER McFALL

Children's Books

THE PILOT'S DAUGHTER

❖❖❖

Poems by

Gardner McFall

TIME BEING BOOKS
POETRY IN SIGHT AND SOUND
St. Louis, Missouri

Time Being Books®
10411 Clayton Road
St. Louis, Missouri 63131

Time Being Books® is an imprint of Time Being Press®
St. Louis, Missouri

Time Being Press® is a 501(c)(3) not-for-profit organization.

Time Being Books® volumes are printed on acid-free paper, and binding materials are chosen for strength and durability.

ISBN 1-56809-028-5 (Hardcover)
ISBN 1-56809-029-3 (Paperback)

Library of Congress Cataloging-in-Publication Data:

McFall, Gardner
    The pilot's daughter : poems / by Gardner McFall.
        p.   cm.
    ISBN 1-56809-028-5 (cloth). — ISBN 1-56809-029-3 (pbk.)
    I. Title.
    PS3563.C3624P5   1996
    811'.54 — dc20   95-47233
                                                                         C I P

Cover art: Winslow Homer, *The White Rowboat: St. Johns River*. Watercolor on paper, 13 1/2 x 19 1/2 ins. Permission courtesy of the Cummer Museum of Art and Gardens, Jacksonville, Florida, bequest of Ninah Cummer, 1958.
Book design and typesetting by Lori Loesche and Cynthia Higgins.
Cover design by Thomas Wharton

Manufactured in the United States of America

First Edition, first printing (May 1996)

Acknowledgments

I am grateful to the editors of the publications where these poems, occasionally in different form, first appeared: *The Agni Review* ("The Pilot's Daughter"); *Columbia: A Magazine of Poetry & Prose* ("Past Union Square"); *Crazyhorse* ("The Air Pilot's Wife" and "Everything You Need"); *The Georgia Review* ("Shadowlawn"); *The Missouri Review* ("Blue Raft," "Field Trip to Fort Story," "Four Corners," "Identity," and "Missing"); *The Nation* ("Meditation on a Child's Lost Sandals" and "Moves"); *The New Yorker* ("Along the St. Johns"); *The New York Times* ("Use for Pain"); *The Paris Review* ("The Encounter" and "Mother Love"); *Pequod* ("Mission in Hong Kong"); *The Poetry Miscellany* ("Expectations" and "Waking at Night"); *Ploughshares* ("After Thanksgiving," "Facts," "Needlepoint," "Peninsular Life," and "Plaint," originally published as "Complaint," and "Recife, the Venice of Brazil"); *Salamander* ("Paradise of Fish"); *The Seattle Review* ("The Boating Party"); *Shenandoah* ("Describing the Middle Ages" and "Over Florida"); *Tendril* ("After the Fairy Tales of Oscar Wilde, Part One"); *Western Humanities Review* ("Leaving Heaven").

"Facts" appeared in the *1984 Anthology of Magazine Verse & Yearbook of American Poetry.* "After the Fairy Tales of Oscar Wilde, Part One" was published as "Sonnet" in *Love Songs for Voice and Piano,* by Daron Hagen, E.C. Schirmer Company, Boston, 1992. "Shadowlawn" was reprinted in *Victoria*, April 1994.

I wish to thank the Corporation of Yaddo and the MacDowell Colony for residencies. For their thoughtful criticism, I'm indebted to Henri Cole, Jane Shore, and Michael J. Rosen.

In memory of my father,
Cdr. A. Dodge McFall, U.S.N.
(1927-1966)

for my mother, and Peter

Pray for the grace of accuracy
Vermeer gave to the sun's illumination
stealing like the tide across a map
to his girl solid with yearning.
We are poor passing facts,
warned by that to give
each figure in the photograph
his living name.
— Robert Lowell, "Epilogue"

But are not all Facts Dreams as soon as we put them behind us?
— Emily Dickinson, from *The Letters of Emily Dickinson*

Contents

THE PILOT'S DAUGHTER

❖❖❖

PROLOGUE

PLAINT

God said He would destroy Earth's violent flesh
but spare me. Was there gratitude enough
for such a burden? My family blessed Him.
They built the Ark according to His dimensions,
cubit by square cubit. He was specific,
demanding gopher wood, three stories pitched within,
one window, and two of every creature.
Opening a door to so many, could I choose
which pairs? I took those near.
The rest, water devoured. I could not behold
the meadowlarks' ascent, though I heard
the rain beating down, their cries, silence.

Awake nights on Ararat, I think He should have
picked another to bear the duplication,
shiny and new, except in memory. Today,
I am sending out the raven and dove over the still,
watery world. The cattle kick their stall.
The mockingbirds have given up their imitations.
I do what I must, but it is unnatural here,
keeping alive so much that wants out. I need
ground to stand on and trees to show me my place.

Part One

ON THE LINE

❖❖❖

OVER FLORIDA

Up here with our obliging stewardess,
everything is provided for.
If emergencies arise, no one can reach us.
In good weather like this,
the Atlantic is breathtaking
or heartbreaking with the pin-size towns
tucked neatly along the threading tributaries
and those grave little dashes of boats.
Stitched inland, the needle-thin railroads
are edged with bunches of nosegay trees.
The ocean looks frozen yet changes color
according to depth. From this vantage,
whether one looks down or not,
the earth is a manageable place,
like the train set we kept in the basement,
our whole world spread on three card tables.
We dismantled it, held each section
of track in one hand, reconstructed it
in the shape of an 8. The bristly, thumb-tall
trees, colored a perennial autumn,
could be planted in back of the church
or in front of the houses, one for each.
The figurines stood just as we placed them,
on their bright lawns admiring fall,
under the station clock, whose movable hands
we turned back for another hour of play.
We didn't think of it as play
but as important business, hauling
livestock to a neighboring town,
halting the trains at their crossings.
We maintained the ties with perfect care.
No car ever derailed along
the blue-felt reversible rivers.
Now, as at the top of the basement stairs,
we begin our approach.
We descend over pine-scrub and palms.

The waves, which were gently affixed
borders of lace, grow raucous again.
The confident boats race away
from the indelible coast.

FIELD TRIP TO FORT STORY

Once, after a northeaster,
my fifth-grade biology class
went to Fort Story, Virginia,
to gather marine life
from the half-submerged rocks.

What wasn't attached to the rocks,
waves had raked to a damp shell-bed.
We marched through spindrift
behind our teacher, sure
as a lighthouse signaling us on.

Occasionally, she'd turn
with a strand of pale egg cases
or the husk of a horseshoe crab.
She intoned parts of the seaweed —
"blade" and "holdfast" — saying

we'd only started to find specimens
indigenous to the region.
After half a mile, we came to
a cargo hull banked in the sand,
within sight of a dune-capped fort.

Out of boredom or interest,
we took turns at the rust-eaten rail
to gaze through a cloudy porthole.
Inside, the chart room's table
stood bolted to the floor.

Across the smooth top,
a sailor's instruments were scattered.
I looked at the compass and log
beside a tipped-over kerosene lamp.
What was the unimaginable

that had brought the ship here?
When our buckets were full,
we filed back to the bus
for our next assignment —
identifying what we'd collected.

Gulfweed, eelgrass, knotted wrack
were mine, mounted on index cards
with phylum, date, and location
inscribed. Through the years,
they've kept their exact color

and sea-scent, preserved
like the vessel we saw grounded,
going nowhere. They recall
that tidewater day as definitive,
like the continental shelf

dividing shallows from the deep —
not knowing how the ocean
casts up without warning
the study of life
from the study of death.

Expectations

When we turned from the cement drive
to the gravel road, I might have expected
anything from my brother, just six,
learning to ride a two-wheeler for the first time.
Older by five years, I ran beside him
like a bedrail to keep him from falling,

while Mother stood on the front stoop,
hands visor-fashion over her eyes.
She looked like a cheerleader fixed on the play.
My father appeared at the road's end,
an imaginary finish line we wavered toward
in a shaky, ongoing S.

Time seemed endless, the moment
between knowing and not knowing whether
he would ride on straight without me,
whether he would spill to the other side
or into my arms. And how could I keep
the world from spinning as the two wheels

turned and kept turning over the stones and dust?
Whatever it was I tripped on, I went down
knee, shoulder, cheek to a quick, clean fracture
of the wrist no one could foresee or accept.
And so I went to bed in the still-light
evening, assured I would be well,

torn between assurance and the small pain
that outgrew my limbs by morning.
Now, it seems slapstick that an older sister
stumbles beside her brother,
but the ground for human error
is immense, and I've since learned

people will tell you
your arm's not broken, not because
they don't want to drive you to the dispensary,
not even because they don't believe
the pain you feel, but, put simply,
it's not supposed to happen like that.

FOUR CORNERS

Two parents in front, two children in back,
driving west in the hottest part of summer.
The dog's ears flapped in the wind.
Nothing could relieve that heat, not even

the soft drinks fished from our ice-chest.
In Kansas we counted the silos and fields;
then, after the Rockies, all the trading posts,
whose outdoor curios and blanket displays

gathered dust from the speeding trucks.
Late afternoon, our interest in scenery
fell on the possibility of a motel pool.
That's when we happened to spot the sign,

Four Corners. We found it described
in *Fodor's Guide*: marked by a low, square
monument, the state lines of Arizona, Utah,
Colorado, and New Mexico meeting in the middle.

It could have been anywhere if you believe
what you read. Hardly anything distinguished
that point where four states touch,
but we stopped the car. A man took our picture

to prove we were there, balanced together
on a concrete slab small as a kitchen table,
shoulder to shoulder, each in a different state,
our hair blowing in the same direction.

MOVES

When the movers leave my mother's china
and linen in the rain in the front yard
of the penultimate place we're stationed,
she sits down among the boxes
scattered like a child's blocks
and says, I'm never moving again.
She's almost right.
There's only one more move, out to Lemoore,
where VA-76 will leave for Vietnam.
And when she gets there,
she wants to go home, suddenly,
where her family is.
So my father drives us 80 miles an hour
cross-country and flies back
to take the squadron on a second tour.
Though he's gone, though he's been gone
more years than he's been at home,
we carry on our ordinary lives.
I wear a sky-dyed uniform each day
to the local school for girls;
my brother joins Cub Scouts.
Mother volunteers at Navy Relief.
When the glossy military car pulls up,
my mother is not home,
not sitting down collected,
but driving up the street
with bags of groceries in the back seat.
And even when she sees it,
she thinks nothing of it.
She thinks it's a social call.
Only when the chaplain gets out
does the thought cross her mind.
Then, she begins to shake.
Grief travels toward you this way
out of the blue. It finds you
unprepared, as when you spy

your mother across the asphalt
basketball court where she's come
to retrieve you from school,
and she puts her arm around you
somewhere between gym and world history
and says, your father is missing.

MISSING

For years I lived with the thought
of his return. I imagined he had ditched
the plane and was living on a distant
island, plotting his way back
with a faithful guide; or, if
he didn't have a guide, he was sending
up a flare in sight of an approaching ship.

Perhaps, having reached an Asian capital,
he was buying gifts for a reunion
that would dwarf the ones before.
He would have exotic stories to tell,
though after a while, the stories
didn't matter or the gifts.

One day I told myself, he is not coming
home, though I had no evidence,
no grave, nothing to say a prayer over.
I knew he was flying among the starry
plankton, detained forever.
But telling myself this was as futile
as when I found a picture of him

sleeping in the ready room,
hands folded across his chest,
exhausted from the sortie he'd flown.
His flight suit was still on,
a jacket collapsed at his feet.
I half thought I could reach out

and wake him, as the unconscious
touches the object of its desire
and makes it live. I have kept
all the doors open in my life
so that he could walk in, unsure
as I've been how to relinquish
what is not there.

FACTS

for my father

In your orange flight suit, you approached the Renault
we knew might stall after a hard winter freeze.
With your pilot's hand, you turned the engine.
When it caught, I ran down the walkway you'd shoveled.

Cinderella lunchbox under my arm, I climbed
in the frozen capsule and waited for you
to clear morning like the path through snow:
hot water on the windshield. Ten below.

We skidded past our milkman, late with deliveries.
The paperboy's bright hand catapulted good-bye.
In your Scottish complexion, I recognized mine,
pink, freckled. Its color dissolved

in the heater's breath. That morning, the scarf
at your neck wound a jet stream like Lindbergh's in Paris,
but the brim of your cap was embroidered with oak leaves,
and stitched on the back, the words "Tonkin Gulf."

When we reached the schoolyard, I told you to take
care, my habit in leave-taking, as if care
were portable or compact like a parachute.
Your car veered toward the airfield and disappeared.

Those facts I have no use for. Twenty years
I dream your death-plane back, down the foggy night,
over the carrier, to the landing deck and hookmen's wire.
You kill the engine. Opening the cockpit,

your hand raises a sign of hello. I keep this picture
for every mission you flew. You are always climbing out
of your plane, its wing flaps down, cool, hangar-bound,
to show me a way, if not around, then through.

THE AIR PILOT'S WIFE

By March we've had our share of rain.
What's the point of living in the South
if you can't count on the weather?
With Easter only a week away,
the azaleas have taken their cue,
and the rosebushes will soon be
a horseshoe of color. I still prefer
yellow ones, though neighbors exclaim
over the new-dawn pink.
Of course, I'll give them some.
Yesterday, a deer and her fawn
came to the edge of the back lot.
They were so attentive to each other,
they didn't notice me.
Their cinnamon bodies were soft
and sleek in the afternoon
sun filtering through the pines.
They are Roman pines, I've discovered.
For a moment, with the light streaming down,
I thought I was in a cathedral.
There was no place to look but up.
When the deer bounded off, it was without
a sound, without disturbing a single
needle or cone. And there are plenty.
I often think of doing something
with the land out back, cultivating it
or building a guest-house,
but it's more nature's than mine.
I like the furrowing moles.
The destructive squirrels and loudmouthed
jays are here. They have their homes,
their mates. They go about their business,
which gives me pleasure.
I have this feeling for the land
which you had for the air,
or perhaps you had a feeling for the land

but from a different perspective.
You saw it day after day
and by night from a great distance.
How small the earth was to you.
I see things closeup.
I would get down on my hands and knees
to glimpse the first hint of iris.
With March arrived, there's all this
quickening. Sometimes,
I just want to talk with you.

PENINSULAR LIFE

Low tide along this oceanfront
there are the usual chipped conchs,
angel wings, Atlantic augers
spiraling to pin tips,
and occasionally, beyond the sea wrack
or tangled in it, a perfect starfish.

Rainbowed donax burrow
at the water's edge, moving
beneath the surface like slippers.
Some escape the sandpipers
which scatter when we head south
toward St. Augustine.

We're used to the sharks' teeth
under our feet, the lazy line
of pelicans, and the pale sea oats
that comb the air.
It's hard to imagine what
we haven't found,

mostly by accident:
the whole, rare sand dollar
bleached to chalk dust
and the whelk whose interior
luster resembles a sunset.

One night, the phosphorus
shone so on the waves,
we watched a large, dark sea turtle
crawl out of the surf
and drag herself over the hard-
packed littoral to pliable sand.

She dug a hole with a kind
of fury, then covered the eggs
before starting back,
her body light again.
She left an imprint of her journey
between the tidal marks.

I know we stood for half an hour
while the waves rolled in and swept
her path away like the close,
salty air at bedtime that sweeps
consciousness from us.
The water rose and tugged our ankles

before we finally moved on.

SHADOWLAWN

When she lived there, I spent afternoons
in the den. Animals and dolls kept house
beneath the chairs and butler's table.
From another room, she carried in magnolia
blossoms, floating in a wide, shallow bowl.

I pressed my nose to the white petals unfolding.
Don't touch, she'd say, they'll yellow.
But folded out, they always turned
the color of iron-scorched linen.

I never saw a flower on that tree for long.
Evenings, she would stand beyond the sprinkler
with her clipping shears, and gloves on.
Grandfather would sit porch-side and look
and look. Was I missing something?

Sometimes a rainbow glimmered
in the thin arcs of water fanning the lawn.
A dog trotted by. Or wind rippled
the Spanish moss like a woman's hair.

Marched through the house, up back stairs
for bath-time, before light had completely fallen
or the jays quieted down, I could still smell
magnolia, as if the sheets had been washed in it.

FOR THE MOMENT

But for the moment, let's calculate
   what we do have: the shady palms
      above us, paradise trees, *bois fidèle,*

a scuffed-up mat of water oak,
   bordergrass with lilac florets lining
      the blue-slate flagstones, or

a walk through America's oldest city,
   where the back streets run off into the heart
      of a grown-up neighborhood

and ocean-bound boats fly past
   the last reach of land, Fort Matanzas.
      Here's the schoolhouse,

restored and painted, a stone's throw
   from where the Fountain of Youth stood,
      a memory now, but that's something, too,

or something else. The sight's just
   relocated up the road. Ponce de León,
      armored head to toe, points the direction.

An authentic conqueror, he built a cross
   where he landed and prayed — thanks, no doubt,
      for having sailed safely so far.

If we stay until nine, cicadas will strike up
   and night-blooming jasmine ignite the air.
      We might see a manatee loll

on her side in the fast, the glimmering water.

ALONG THE ST. JOHNS

The purple hyacinths, flamboyant wafers,
float between the river pilings. The pelicans
circle in a ritual breakfast flight.
Most of the docks are caving into the silken,
oil-flecked water, but the outdated drawbridge
crosses the river. The tender's station perched
high on the bridge looks closed as a shop.

Along the St. Johns, with flags and full rigging,
an improbable schooner clangs an unholy bell.
The drawbridge honors it with halting labor,
raising its arms to the tall, lean mast,
but not quite fast enough. The boat cuts its motor.
It churns nervously backward, perfectly dependent
on the old racks and pinions and drawbridge tender.

After four or five minutes, the bascules lumber up.
Steep in the air, they stand free as columns
of an ancient temple. The schooner sails down
the deep-blue corridor, its wide wake leaving two
halves of the river to weave and reweave themselves
under the cross the bridge makes with water,
where pelicans are riding contentedly filled.

Parade Ground

The black and white days are gone.
The green parade ground is blank
where midshipmen marched like wind-up toys,
their caps shellacked and bright as sails.
The flagpole knocks. A loose canopy

flaps over the empty reviewing stands.
Decorous wives of the captains have left.
The chairs are folded and kindling-stacked.
Only the monuments can endure the weather:
Tecumseh the chief, the iron anchor,

and the tomb with the body of John Paul Jones.
The black and white are gone like headlines.
Tears for "America" and the "Navy Hymn"
are packed in a cruise box under a flight jacket
with the days of right and the days of wrong.

The Severn idles near the parade ground.
The cherry and apple trees have started to bloom
along the road that runs to the cemetery,
then up the hill to the house where they lived
and looked out over a country turning thankless.

ON THE LINE

The line where you were,
like the equator, divided the world
in two. Whatever the latitude,
the planes roared off the carrier.
Their bombs fell vertically
on target. In a letter, you wrote:

"Each day we bomb the Ho Chi Minh Trail,
they reconstruct it by night.
We can't win, but don't quote me."
You were a kind man.
You loved your family.
For years I've tried to figure

what you loved more —
not the military life with tours of duty
or the jungle war. You loved
Duty itself, a word, an abstraction.
Now our lines of communication
are cut, except for your blood in me.

These words, strange as your death,
fall as on foreign villages,
unpronounceable names,
all lost on American ears.
I am traveling fast, propelled
by you, doing what I must,
ready to answer for it.

Part Two

TRAVELING

❖❖❖

PARADISE OF FISH

after William Bartram

Walking by the lake with my friend,
remarking the water's clarity,
how the fish jet through
the mirrored clouds and trees,
I think of the salt springs
west of Florida's Lake George,
which gush tons of water each day,
like an enormous heart,
into a pool reflective as ether.
Bands of bream thrive there,
and the normally voracious crocodile
stretches docile as a tree trunk
alongside the trout. Because the water
is translucent, predator and preyed upon
alike have no place to hide.
Circling that basin, they figure
the peaceable kingdom.
They are not even afraid of people.
At first the fish will appear
at a vast distance,
no bigger than minnows or flies,
but gradually they enlarge,
their colors filling the water.
They rise — some upright,
one or two suffering toward the surface.
They descend to rejoin their tribes.
When I feel I could touch
one of these fish without difficulty
or draw close to the crocodile,
I know what it was before the Fall.
It was like this water
where the trout moves freely
by the crocodile's nose,
the bream by the trout's.

THE PILOT'S DAUGHTER

In the twilight I am fishing
from the train trestle
with a friend and my father,
our lines trailing the Chesapeake.
We have stood a good hour
and caught nothing,
until I pull from the depths
a black eel,
whose slithery, hard body
thumps and will not lie flat.

He is three feet long
with gun-metal eyes.
He coils and snaps. So I fall back,
while my friend, with a fast hand,
unhinges the torn mouth
and hacks him in two.
For her, my father has praise.

Walking home in the dark,
I relive the evening.
When I lie down at night,
the eel thrashes above my head.
I take him between my hands
for a brilliant electrocution.
We rise, leaving my father
utterly amazed.
I thought I would do anything
to please him.

If he returned from the deep
Pacific, if he towered over me
in his military whites
demanding courage,
I would say I face what I can,
hauling up this part of me
to examine closely,
circling and circling,

until I free it to the cold, gray bay.

After the Fairy Tales of Oscar Wilde

for Peter

1

Loving the idea of love, a nightingale
pressed her breast to the thorn of a rosebush
so a rose might bloom as red as her blood.
The harder she pressed, the sweeter she sang,
until in the purest ecstasy of song,
her heart and the thorn of the rosebush met.
A man picked the rose for a woman he loved,
but the woman disdained it. The man discarded
the rose near the wheels of a cart. He went
back to his books. He forgot about love
with a valid excuse. Love, let us be neither
the man nor woman but the nightingale:
the sharper the pain, the greater the song,
the deeper the red — the miraculous blossom.

2

When the fisherman saw the mermaid asleep
in his net, he thought he had found
his greatest fortune, finer than a thousand
ocean tunnies, prettier than any girl
in the taverns. As she sang of the sea-green
depths, full of sirens, mariners, mermen,
his only dream was how to possess her.
If you care to win me, she said, *you must lose your soul.*
What good is my soul? the fisherman asked.
I can't see or touch it. Love's much better.
So he stood on the beach, his back
to the full moon. With a knife he cut away
the shadow that housed his soul.
He heard it cry and slip out over the marshes.

3

Haven't we played the twisted dwarf, lacking
a sense of proportion, dancing for all
we were worth before the dainty infanta?
Haven't we been she in a royal, blue gown,
hiding dreamy-eyed behind a pink, gauze fan,
leaning forward on tiptoe, flirting
without feeling for the love-struck dancer?
When the dwarf looks in the palace mirror
and, repulsed by his image, falls to the floor,
the vexed infanta exits, muttering,
Henceforth, let no heart enter here.
That's when I call out, *Children! Get up!*
Come back! Don't be misled by beauty.
Goodness is more precious, dependable, rare.

4

Who would have called them a likely match —
the swallow and gilded statue of the Happy Prince?
Yet the prince's lament surprised the swallow,
who thought he was just a handsome statue:
All day I stand surveying the city, and all I see
is the city's poor. The swallow was moved to be
his emissary, pluck the ruby from the prince's sword,
carry his sapphire eyes and armor's filigree
to anyone he found starving or cold.
Rather than leave the prince's side, the swallow
froze. When town councilors discovered
the ugly statue, they ordered him to be melted down,
but his leaden heart, which had split in two,
would not burn, so much had it been a heart of love.

THE BOATING PARTY

after Mary Cassatt

It is impossible to say whether the figures
seated in the boat are moving toward land or away.
The wind is up. The man grips the oars.
The woman in the bow holds their baby boy
on her lap. I think it is a boy,
though he wears a striped, pink frock.
His beret resembles his father's.
His shoes are brown, possibly orthopedic.

The eyes speak for the people here.
The baby glances everywhere, unfocused,
as he twists in his mother's arms.
The man and woman stare at each other
as if there were no other landscape,
no red-tiled roofs dotting the distant,
tree-lined Antibes shore and no birds
which undoubtedly fly above them.

Azure water frames their faces.
Their bodies are contained
in so small a space; the boat is falling
out of the picture. Surely, they are connected
by more than the baby between them.
She is sitting there, isn't she?
He is rowing in the manner of courtship.
For an instant, they appear to know

nothing of sadness. They do not estimate
the inclemencies that could flood
their boat or topple it.
They do not realize they are merely
a painting in the National Gallery
which men and women gaze at
for a moment, before returning home,
where life so rarely approaches art.

THE VINTAGERS

Just south of the castle ruin, the *vendange* begins.
October shimmers beneath the fog in Touraine,
too early for the sun. In the dew-starred field
where row after row fans open, the vintagers gather
with baskets and scissors. Clipping the vines' color,
they stand waist-high in a luscious tangle of grapes.

A small cluster fills one woman's hand, but the grapes
hold strong on their stems. They slowly begin
to weaken and fall. Her palm turns violet, a colored
blotter against the heart of Touraine.
She works near a man and moves to keep warm, gathering
her basketful from the heavy, sweet field.

With a wooden pannier strapped to his shoulders, a field-
hand maneuvers through the channels of grapes
to collect what the man and the woman have gathered,
fruit they can never own. By midday, they begin
to grow accustomed to this, weary beneath Touraine's
hot sun but hypnotized by the undulant color

stretching as far as Saumur. His eyes, a colorist's
azure, are as natural and close as sky above the field.
At lunch, he talks of other harvests in Touraine.
They share bread and drink the wine of grapes
reaped there. Not fluent in his language, she begins
to understand phrases. Each word he offers, she gathers

and repeats. In the hours left, she gathers
more than fruit. Its stain discolors
her fingers. Tendrils cut her hands. As sunset begins,
they stack their baskets in the wide, clean field.
Above the rims of large, round tubs, the grapes
glisten, until night's tarpaulin covers Touraine.

Alone at morning, she will travel out of Touraine,
not as she found the valley when they first gathered
nor as they found each other but with the vineyard grapes
perfectly garnered, on her hands their indelible color.
She lingers along the perimeter of empty field
whose dark abundance caused the harvest to begin.

This is Touraine's season of profit, when all color
is gathered with harvesters from the field,
the grapes are pressed, and winter begins.

USE FOR PAIN

I carry mine invisible in these arms
but with the difficulty I might have
bringing firewood or a bag of groceries.

You are as clever at the hearth as you are
in the kitchen. And where I stand at the door
I cannot see yours, if you have any.

Describing the Middle Ages

Although we harbor a look of freedom
and longing, we are not free,

though we climb the circular stairs
to lassitude in each other's arms.

I unbind my hair,
and you abandon your dragon days.

I have decided to show you the gift
of pity, knowing that when we are sated,

when we can bear the difficult beauty
no longer, you will travel away.

You will leave to perform great deeds
in my memory. This is all in a book

describing the middle ages, years
between darkness and light,

lasting a long time, where the vines
grow up over the window casings

high in the turret, and the armor glints
from a corner where it's been thrown,

and far off the wealthy merchant to whom
the lady is married rides homeward,

having inspected his distant estates
and found them all prospering.

LAKE POEMS

1

Night domes the lake we walk around.
We trust the million seining stars
that pull the drowning moon along.
The treetops candling up flare
black, tossed like buoys before a storm.
Must we reinvent daylight's path,
or can we permit some awkward stumbling
that accompanies the dark, the other?
Above, there is a swift flapping,
the bat's high, almost human pitch.
The limned embankment holds the first
of the season's glowworms, soft and steady
as a pulse. The space between us weighs
no more than a net we might cast out
together. Rising within the woods,
the crying bird's strain warns
of our approach, the possibilities of danger.

2

This morning I saw the periscopic turtle
bank on a log, turquoise dragonflies
tip the lake, gnats bob on invisible strings.
A mallard called from some distant edge.
I remained still in my own reflections,
observing the dark center, the light-
filled shallows, the wind scaling the surface
or scattering a hundred flecks. The fish
torpedoed on their rounds, shadows
among shadows. Images superimposed
themselves like feelings — tree upon cloud
upon water upon fish. All that is
certain is that the water is green
because green trees encircle it,

the water that absorbs everything
and gives it back like a looking glass
or a room of perfect acoustics,
your eyes, the breadth of your arms.

3

I left first, but not even you are there now.
Mid-July, the water lilies have turned
from bedsheet white to year-old news;
the lake has assumed a new texture
and shade, like the morning we saw
showers suddenly displace the green,
turning the lake overcast.
So the days of constant sun layer
the untended water with torpid algae,
making the clarity difficult to recall.
I am thinking of the philosopher
who said "Solitude has several skins.
Nothing can penetrate it,"
and a painter who built his sanctuary
from art. While the heat crouches
on every fire escape in the city,
my fan creates the illusion of wind.

THE ENCOUNTER

The burnt-red fox darts in front
of the car's path late at night,
and I'd like to call this an encounter,

though all I really catch is its pointed
tail tip, white in the headlights.
The nearly full moon glows

like an unexpected touch
or only the thought hovering
between what if and why not.

I'd like to say the fox came back
and danced its fox dance just for me,
and after I stopped the car and got out,

it put its fox face in my hand, trusting
I would not startle or offend
but understand the risk it had taken,

moving out of the shadows, crossing
the grass and gravel between us.
Not that I would become fox or it human.

It is never a question of that,
but I would honor the difference,
the strange gift abandon brings.

Mission in Hong Kong

I looked for you
in the harbor's blue water.
I looked to see
if a carrier was in.
I looked for you
in the neon signs;
perhaps they were here then.

I went to the Star Ferry.
I walked in Victoria Park.
Did I see what you saw —
people taking their caged finches
for air? I traveled by tram
to Victoria Peak, spotted
the Hong Kong Hilton

where you stayed —
I went there.
I went to some bars.
I looked for you
in Kowloon and found
replicas of the gifts
you bought: porcelain cats,

a carved water buffalo.
I ate in a restaurant
you might have known.
I looked for you in the faces
of men on leave. I looked
for you in the streets
whose names I could not read.

My husband said to meet him
at Maiwo Yang, a tailor
who had made him a suit.
Maiwo Yang — the tag sewn
in your white shirt I wore
until I wore it away.
I ran as fast as I could.

I tried to note everything —
the weather, the hour, the steps
to the door, emblazoned with
"Woolen Merchants & Tailors."
"Where is Mr. Maiwo Yang?" I asked.
Behind the racks of suits I found him.
"My father was here in 1966."

He smiled vaguely — my story
nothing new — and then,
with pins between his teeth,
resumed altering a trouser cuff,
bolts of nautical blue
adrift at his feet, from which
he might have cut a uniform for you.

RECIFE, THE VENICE OF BRAZIL

Our guide has built our hopes up.
He claims Recife is the Venice
of Brazil, but nothing so far
in the state of Pernambuco
equals the Grand Canal
or the Doge's Palace.
Where are the gondolas
and glassblowers?

Our guide insists. He drives us
over "Venetian-like" bridges,
and each bridge leads
to a Moorish church on the edge
of town, more than a dozen,
all built to commemorate
deliverance from the Dutch.
Every time-rubbed tympanum
is an unreadable scene,
the altars flanked
by primitive statues of saints.

Outside, between churches,
we tour the fields of stricken
sugarcane. Is this what
the Portuguese fought for?
We turn abruptly down a road
for carts, where the men who cut sugarcane
live in flamingo shacks.
Our guide parks
near a palm-thatched awning
so we can taste sugarcane juice
through a handmade straw.
Sickening sweet, it is
thicker than medicine.

But I am polite,
balancing on rinds and coconuts
close to what must be
the jungle. Can we go now?
There's more?
We head toward the jetty.
At the tip, some fishing rods
wedged between the rocks
lean toward a reef
where waves are breaking.
Our guide says the city roads
ran beyond there once,
but the sea was hungry for houses.

Like Venice.
Seeing us, the fishermen hold up
their catch, stringers of fish
flecked with a scaly gemstone,
reflecting the sun,
which is poised on the horizon
like a Brazilian topaz,
fit for the doge himself.

LEAVING HEAVEN

After a while, we tired of it,
sitting around in robes
that never soiled or needed an iron.
We remembered rather fondly
the irritating wrinkle,
the pleasing crease.

The air felt too close,
without a caress or sting.
We wanted to sneeze at a breath
of pollen, signaling flowers,
grass to be mown,
honeysuckle studded with bees.

We wanted control of our culinary
destiny, though we had no need
of food. There was singing,
which sounded fine at first
but soon grew too constant,
too perfectly pitched.

We recalled our earthly voices
that cracked or sang off-key.
In the choir, we wanted to have
some feeling for each other,
whether vicious or tender,
a release from perpetual calm.

The absence of pain
we thought we desired
paled under the proximity of stars,
which is why, though it's hard
to imagine among all those
peerless, ideal clouds,

we wanted to board
the Lucky Streak Greyhound
and set off for the bumpy road,
to see the red geraniums
carefully planted
by the tollbooth once again.

Part Three

NEW GROUND

❖❖❖

Needlepoint

The yarn pulled diagonally
over neighboring threads
in time might equal the sheen
on a bird's feather,
a flower petal's tip,

or some corner of sky.
As far back as I remember,
she was never without
some neutral canvas,
rectangle, circle, square,

her hands having chosen
the continental, basket-weave,
or half-stitch. I watched
to see what design would emerge,
while she sat silently

filling in the outlines,
following a pattern
someone else had painted.
Knotted, bright skeins,
a rainbow, fell from

her chair. Each strand,
with its number corresponding
to dye, in turn matched
a colored block on the inter-
locking mesh. She worked

exactly, like Penelope
weaving her life, driving
her feelings with the blunt
needle inward. If I longed
for concrete evidence of her

not as a mother but as a person,
how could this have escaped
my attention? If I ever thought
we were not alike,
don't I find myself sitting,

connecting words, attempting
to make some picture complete?
And isn't this why
I scan the needlepoint
pillows about the house —

in order to detect
the worry in a flower's stem,
the anger in a bird,
the enormous affection
tinging the off-white clouds?

BLUE RAFT

for my daughter

The first month you floated in me
at the beach of my childhood,
the sun burned my shoulders.
Black crows appeared
among the sandpipers and gulls.
The crows were the only darkness,
out of place with their splayed crow feet,
unable to run or dive like sea-birds.
I watched them on the shore,
donax in their sharp beaks.
I couldn't say whether theirs
was a taste born of necessity or desire.
One looked at me with its hard, berry eyes,
and I looked back,
each of us suspecting the other.
Then, I took the blue raft
from summers before and went out
beyond the waves to flutter-kick and drift.
The ocean was smooth as a platter,
strewn with stars.
I wanted to drift for hours
in forgetful peace,
right into oblivion,
with only the ocean to buoy me
and no one in the houses to call me.
The houses seemed very small
and far away.
When I drifted close to the shrimpers,
a shrill whistle woke me.
I was out too far.
I started to paddle and kick.
All the while I thought of you
floating inside me.
Out too far, out too far.
At last I reached the point

where waves swell,
and a wave lifted the raft
high, then down.
The foam enveloped me
the way it would when I'd ride
on my father's back,
a knapsack, a small burden
among salty pleasure.
I skidded over the broken shells
to ankle-deep water, and as I rose,
taking the blue raft lightly under my arm,
salt and sand clinging to me,
I thought of how my father would say,
lying on a raft in the Atlantic,
"This is the life." He was dead,
but you were floating in me,
and the crows, like some new part
of myself, stood on the beach,
exquisitely black, shining.

Mother Love

Strollers, diapers, bottles overwhelm
the young mother in the nether reaches
of life after birth no one told her about,
not in the pregnancy class where she learned
labor breathing or at the baby shower
where gifts accumulated like drifts:
blankets, crib sheets, bumpers.
It would take months shoveling out,
sifting her story from others',
her wishes and needs from the inherited
myth that she was made for this,
while he was made to traffic
in the world, conduct business lunches,
and travel in the name of providing,
as though the only provisions were those
to be purchased with a large check.
She must be always giving
and content pushing a little stone
up the hill every day
or sitting with women strung out
on park benches, their minds tethered
to their carriages, their mouths locked.
If only someone might admit
the tedium, she thinks as she stands by the sink
in the settling afternoon sun
and hears a deafening cry erupt
from the other room. She is lost
in the project of motherhood now
and all that is taboo to speak about
and feels as she moves without will
down the hall to gather her child up
fiercely, feels suddenly the impact —
she would kill or be killed for it.
For whom else would she do that?

IDENTITY

Out for a woodsy walk
with a thick cross-hatch
of pine and birch above,
a view of no further

than three yards ahead,
I stumble on a thick
feather bed of ferns,
a sea of downy-green.

Clustered and tossed
like beautiful, careless
clothes, warm dreamers
in abandoned sleep,

unharmed for a time,
they turn and lightly
brush against my legs —
all different kinds

to thrill a collector's
heart. I bend, trying
to salvage what I can
from camp's nature class,

the broad morphology
of fern: rootstock, stem,
and frond; each leaflet
branching from the delicate

axis divisible into sub-
leaflet, lobe, teeth.
The undulating bracken
and singular hart's-tongue,

the tangled, tissue-thin
maidenhair are those
I recall; also (I'd forgotten
until now) the common

polypody once pressed
in a book. Small, evergreen,
and vigorous, a mantle
to rocks and trees,

here its winged, blunt-
tipped, leathery leaflets
rise out of an old log,
Thoreau's "fresh, cheerful

communities"; and more —
incapable of being
any kind of fern
but the one it is.

EVERYTHING YOU NEED

Some days the world is simply what it is,
but you have everything you need.
The shady meadow with its stream welcomes you,
and the provisions in the picnic basket
are beyond belief.

That is in one country.
In another, it rains.
Instead of the magic of cuckoos,
there is the droning traffic,
too little time, all badly spent.
And the person you thought you were traveling with
is nowhere in sight.

But you can remember
how the light lingered.
The earth resembled a masterpiece,
and you were in it,
amazed by your good fortune,
the way you felt amazed
to touch the charred lantern
somebody carried on the crusades
and the wooden trunk
packed with their worldly goods.
They'd be buried in it
if they died at sea.

The trunk hardly seemed real.
It was small as a trinket,
though it was somebody's treasure
and somebody's grief.

PAST UNION SQUARE

During the night the wind spins down yellow ginkgo leaves
like bits of paper. This time of year, we raked
the small front yard clean of accumulated oak, maple,
and whatever else the weather dislodged.

In a city almost void of nature, a single leaf impression
underfoot is enough to spark this thought:
it took the entire afternoon before a bonfire expressed
our labor, in one long blaze, running like a shared sigh

from the earth. I don't know why, besides habit,
we bothered at all, since in a month or two
the snow settled everything.
This morning I walk from my apartment toward work,

past Union Square and its military statue,
which permanently rides beneath the bare ginkgo trees.
Maintenance men spear trash and move on.
But the ginkgo leaves, whose delicate fan shape in spring

now resembles the bell of a brass horn, remain
strewn in the burnished light, the kind of light
one sees in turn-of-the-century photographs,
and I see now, holding this leaf in my palm,

remembering: I stood transfixed in the November air.
I was sweater-layered under pinpoint stars,
saying Father or Mother still, calling my brother's name
when it was time to walk back to the house.

AFTER THANKSGIVING

After Thanksgiving, what is there
but old newspaper and wet leaves pressed
on the drive? We step out
onto the road, glistening like blue coal,
and can walk for miles.

The doctor next door stands in his yard,
hands to hips, surveying Spanish moss
the limbs wrenched out of the sky.
A dog wags his melancholy tail.
How the world can be so still, earth holding

us in its breath, and you concerned
the name *earth* is not sonorous enough
to impress an alien planet.
Dirt, road, woods
are never what they sound like.

Ages from now and miles, this will be
our neighborhood speaking for itself:
catbirds gone crazy in rain pools,
squirrels scratching through trees,
children splashing up water with their bikes.

All we are missing is a solitary mower
carving out the afternoon.
But it gets colder. Whatever we call our world,
in a minute it might snow,
the dog decide to bark.

Waking at Night

All night I listen to your steady breathing
the way I listened for the hall clock
as a child. Its stroke rocked me to sleep.
I woke at morning without considering
who wound it or cleaned its glass,
shut tight over small black numerals.
How easily I slept by that clock,
unaware of its claim on me, its low voice
inscrutable as stars saying sleep, sleep.

Tonight, wakened by the rhythm of your breath,
the frailest report of the heart,
I walk back and forth in our living room.
Generations fill this house with armoire,
porcelain, hall clock. There's nothing
we haven't inherited. For a second,
time and love converge, while outside
the slight moon slips down the windless sky
over what is impossible to retrieve.

MAGIC FINGERS

The mechanical horse that canters
in place to William Tell
is what my daughter likes best,
headed home up Broadway
after a day spent
at the Museum of Natural History.

She knows each shop-door ride:
duck, sports car, toad.
Each costs a quarter,
though she stops beside
her favorite and begs a penny.
Sometimes I say I don't have one

or I'm saving my quarters
for laundry, but to her surprise
today, I produce a coin from my bag.
She takes it, climbs aboard,
and sets off in her own world
of danger and delight, gripping

the reins of her dark Appaloosa,
then letting go, hands in the air.
I shift from one foot
to the other, feeling foolish,
unable to enter her simple glee;
her brief ride has the weight

of forever as the trumpeting
overture starts again.
Really, there's no difference
between her joy and mine
when I was slightly older than she
and every Holiday Inn

my family stopped at
had a small, metallic bedside
box called "Magic Fingers."
Would the fingers shake my body
or stroke my back
like an indulgent parent?

Maybe the mattress would open
like doors, and I'd fall through.
It was worth the money, I thought.
So, before a dip in the pool
or dinner, before we'd unpacked
for the night, I'd take a quarter

and lie down on the bed
in an attitude of prayer
or death, all expectation —
easily met. I had no idea
the hardly perceptible movement,
the soundless back and forth —

more like a drawer pulled out
from the bureau, then closed —
was what I'd experience
the first time I loved a man,
then had to ask when it was over.
For now, my daughter outruns

every disappointment
on her stationary steed.
As music chimes in our ears,
I slip another quarter in
before she asks, and the years
carry her away from me.

FOURTH OF JULY, PONTE VEDRA

Most of us are jaded now.
Tonight's frisson derives from too much sun,
though when somebody says it's nine o'clock,
we hurry to the lawn and rearrange
Adirondack chairs facing the fireworks.

The first one cracks like a whip
as though something's failed,
then opens into a bold chrysanthemum,
the color of syrup, pouring
and pouring over the waffle sea.

We all emit some blasé oohs and ahs,
but you, unchastened by what's not real,
appear thunderstruck, pointing
a finger skyward, calling us
to attend in ways we've forgotten.

We adults decide to play a Rorschach game
to make the display bearable:
a field of poppies, someone says.
A diamond crown. A tangle of grapes,
dropping one by one. Not too much that's original.

You, however, are transfixed in the grass,
intent on the next miraculous burst.
Inside, the dog's run under the bed.
Come, sit in my arms, little one.
Remember for some future night down the years,

you thought this spinning pinwheel everything.

Meditation on a Child's Lost Sandals

Buoyant as breath
released underwater,
the rainbow jellies,
designed to float,

possibly thrilled,
cut loose from earth
into another element,
not to keep running

over sand and bulkhead
flattening their soles,
but free of the foot's
contour, learning

the dips and peaks
of waves, washed
by a new transport.
All possibility lay

in the tidal hand
that opened and closed
with impudent speed,
discriminating —

whatever fell
beyond reach or weighed
too much stayed.
Let the adventure begin,

drummed the waves,
ferrying them off
to the middle of things,
rocked, flung

along the beachfront,
then dropped
a few houses down —
still a pair — for the small,

grieving owner to find
and claim a miracle,
which, truly, it seemed,
since there can be

no accounting for what
the tide takes and returns
along this lengthening
shore of loss and grace.

EPILOGUE

MY DAUGHTER'S COLLAGE

A tailored blue-jay feather here
    beside a tassel of fresh pine,
the plush-white, speckled, fan-shaped
    souvenir of an unidentified bird,
a three-leaf clover green as luck,
    two twirling maple pods, a fern,
all gathered up, glued down
    in some arrangement of the world

preserved on cardboard.

May life, for her, repeat this art,
    whatever is natural and good
be hers, whatever falls be reassembled
    in some pleasing, individual
form. Compensation? Perhaps,
    and the will to bend when necessary
combined with a wish to build
    something entire from parts

continuing: a rich, singular texture.

Biographical Note

Gardner McFall was born in Jacksonville, Florida, in 1952. She holds a bachelor's degree from Wheaton College (Massachusetts), a master's degree from the Writing Seminars at The Johns Hopkins University, and a doctorate in English from New York University. She received the *Missouri Review's* Thomas McAfee Prize for poetry in 1987 and a "Discovery"/*The Nation* award in 1989. Author of the children's books *Jonathan's Cloud* (Harper & Row, 1986) and *Naming the Animals* (Viking, 1994), Ms. McFall teaches literature at The Cooper Union in New York City. She lives in New York with her husband and daughter.

Also available from **Time Being Books**

LOUIS DANIEL BRODSKY
You Can't Go Back, Exactly
The Thorough Earth
Four and Twenty Blackbirds Soaring
Mississippi Vistas: Volume One of *A Mississippi Trilogy*
Falling from Heaven: Holocaust Poems of a Jew and a Gentile
    (with William Heyen)
Forever, for Now: Poems for a Later Love
Mistress Mississippi: Volume Three of *A Mississippi Trilogy*
A Gleam in the Eye: Poems for a First Baby
Gestapo Crows: Holocaust Poems
The Capital Café: Poems of Redneck, U.S.A.
Disappearing in Mississippi Latitudes:
    Volume Two of *A* Mississippi Trilogy
Paper-Whites for Lady Jane: Poems of a Midlife Love Affair

HARRY JAMES CARGAS (Editor)
Telling the Tale: A Tribute to Elie Wiesel on the Occasion of His
    65th Birthday — Essays, Reflections, and Poems

JUDITH CHALMER
Out of History's Junk Jar: Poems of A Mixed Inheritance

GERALD EARLY
How the War in the Streets Is Won: Poems on the Quest of Love
    and Faith

ALBERT GOLDBARTH
A Lineage of Ragpickers, Songpluckers, Elegiasts & Jewelers:
    Selected Poems of Jewish Family Life (1973–1995)

ROBERT HAMBLIN
From the Ground Up: Poems of One Southerner's Passage to
    Adulthood

TIME BEING BOOKS
POETRY IN SIGHT AND SOUND
St. Louis, Missouri

FOR OUR FREE CATALOG OR TO ORDER
(800) 331-6605 • (314) 432-1771
FAX: (314) 432-7939

PENGUIN BOOKS

A COMPANION TO *THE GRAPES OF WRATH*

Warren French has taught at Kansas State University, University of Mississippi, University of Kentucky, and University of Florida. His articles have appeared widely, and he is the author of *John Steinbeck, Frank Norris,* and *J. D. Salinger,* all in the Twayne United States Authors Series.